# GREAT
# WORLD LEADERS
## THEIR LIVES AND CONTRIBUTIONS

Lee Kheng Chooi

PARTRIDGE

**To order additional copies of this book, contact**
Toll Free 800 101 2657 (Singapore)
Toll Free 1 800 81 7340 (Malaysia)
orders.singapore@partridgepublishing.com

www.partridgepublishing.com/singapore

# CONTENTS

# INTRODUCTION

For years people debated whether leaders are born or made. One school of thought advocates that leaders such as Winston Churchill and Abraham Lincoln are the selected few born with predisposed genetics to be leaders as if they were preordained. The other school of thought advocates that anyone can grow, learn, and develop into a leader.

Warren Bennis, whom Forbes once referred to as the 'professor of leadership gurus,' was an author and ex-adviser to four U.S. presidents, including John F. Kennedy and Ronald Reagan. Bennis said that after spending time observing leaders and leadership closely that it is a myth that leaders are born with a genetic factor to lead. He concludes that anyone who has the desire to learn through hard work, focused effort, and consistent action has the potential to be a great leader.

Whether you believe leaders are born or leaders are made, we know one thing for sure -they come in all shapes and sizes. Their leadership style can range from charismatic to inspiring, and their personalities can differ from energetic to intense. Either way, many of these great leaders left their mark on the world.

In this book, we will explore some of the prominent leaders - giving you an insight into their lives and contributions to the world. Perhaps reading this book will help you in your self-discovery, be it in finding your own purpose, a commitment to learning, or simply expressing your unique gifts. The bottom line is that all of us can learn something from these great leaders before us.

*"Leaders are not born or made. They are self-made." -Stephen Covey*

# CHAPTER 1
# MAHATMA GANDHI

*"The best way to find yourself is to lose yourself in the service of others." - Mahatma Ghandhi*

**12 February 1809 - 15 April 1865**

<u>Early life</u>

Mahatma Gandhi was born in Porbandar, India. His father, Karamchand, was the chief minister of Porbandar state. Gandhi's mother, Putlibai, was a religious woman steeped in Vaishnavism - the worship of the Hindu god, Vishnu. As a result, Gandhi grew up accustomed to fasting, vegetarianism, and tolerance for other sects and creeds.

<u>Education & marriage</u>

Ghandhi studied at the local school near his home and was a good student. He was said to be shy, often preferring to read his books or attend school lessons.

At thirteen, Gandhi was married to fourteen-year-old, Kasturbai Makhanji Kapadia through an arranged marriage. In 1885, Gandhi's father passed away, and the couple had their first child who died a few days later. They eventually had four sons.

In 1887, Gandhi graduated from high school and enrolled for college at Bhavnagar state but dropped out later. At eighteen, Gandhi left for London to study law for three years at the University of London. During his time in London, Gandhi struggled to adapt to the Western ways, and his vegetarianism was a source of embarrassment to him until he joined a vegetarian society. Around this time, he translated the classic Hindu literature Bhagavad Gita and read the Bible - both of which stuck with him throughout his life.

<u>Early career</u>

In 1891, Gandhi returned to India with his barrister's degree, but the legal profession was already overcrowded. He could only find work drafting petitions for litigants. In 1893, Gandhi accepted a job in Natal (now KwaZulu-Natal), South Africa, where he spent the next twenty-one years. During this time, he was struck by the injustice and racial discrimination experienced by Indians, such as not being allowed to travel in first class on the train. It was in South Africa that Gandhi developed into a proficient political campaigner as he overcame his fear of giving speeches and addressing crowds. Meanwhile, Gandhi was also imprisoned several times as he experimented with his non-violent campaigns and protests.

Political career

In 1915, Gandhi returned to India and later became the leader of the thirty-five-year-old Indian National Congress, which he reorganized into an effective political tool of Indian nationalism. His main program was the non-violent movement against the British government, which included boycotts of the British and their counterparts, operated manufactures, and institutions.

In 1930, Gandhi led his most famous and successful march to the sea to protest against the new salt laws by the British. Despite over 300 hundred protesters being beaten and 60,000 people being imprisoned by the British, they did not put up any resistance. In 1931, Gandhi was invited to London to begin a three months talk with the British government led by Lord Irwin. This resulted in the Gandhi-Irwin Pact, whereby the British agreed to release all political prisoners in return for calling off civil disobedience. During this trip, Gandhi was heavily opposed and criticized by Winston Churchill, who called him a dictator, preying on the ignorance of his people for selfish gain. Churchill also called him a half-naked fakir for wearing his traditional Indian dress to visit the King of England. To which Gandhi humorously replied, the king was wearing enough clothes for both of them.

In December 1931, the British imprisoned Gandhi in the hope of isolating him from his followers. While still imprisoned in 1932, Gandhi embarked on a fast to protest against the British government's decision to segregate the untouchables known as the lowest level of the Indian caste system.

In 1934, Gandhi resigned as the leader of the congress party to focus on building the country from the bottom up through education. He moved to Sevagram, a village in central India, which became the center of his social and economic outreach.

## India independence

In 1939, Gandhi opposed India's participation in World War II, but over 2.5 million Indians still joined the British military. As the war progressed, he intensified his Quit India Movement to demand independence. The British responded by imprisoning Gandhi and his congressmen in 1942. During his two years of arrest, Gandhi's wife died after eighteen months of his imprisonment while he suffered from malaria. In 1944, Gandhi was released on account of his ailing health.

Finally, toward the end of the war, the British indicated that they would give India its independence. However, India would be partitioned into India and Pakistan. Gandhi opposed the segregation and worked hard to prove that Hindus and Muslims could coexist peacefully. Unfortunately, even his appeals and fasting could not prevent the violence and sectarian killings that followed the partition.

## Death

Gandhi, seventy-eight years old, undertook his last fasting to prevent the sectarian killing. On his way to a prayer meeting, he was shot by a Hindu fanatic who opposed his support for the untouchables and Muslims. Gandhi's death was mourned nationwide, and over a million people joined the funeral procession. Ultimately, his death helped garner support for the congress party, which formed the new government and made some 200,000 arrests.

## The man himself

India had just celebrated Mahatma Gandhi's 150 birth anniversary in 2019. Gandhi was the first person to apply the principle of non-violence and peaceful resistance to politics on a massive scale. Today, he remains an inspiration not only for India but for the world -as the man himself once said, "His life is his message." In his autobiography, Gandhi explained that his concept of non-violence is about observing respect toward all living beings in thoughts, words, and actions. Gandhi often used fasting as a political tool, and observers said that his fasting and vegetarianism were also part of his practice in self-restraint and healthy living. As a man, he advocated religious understanding and often sought inspiration from different religions such as Christianity, Buddhism, Hinduism, Islam, and Jainism.

# CHAPTER 2
# WINSTON CHURCHILL

---

**30 November 1874 - 24 January 1965**

<u>Early life</u>

Winston Leonard Churchill was born in Blenheim Palace in Oxfordshire, England. His father was Lord Randolph Churchill and his mother, Jeanette Jerome, an American socialite. Churchill grew up in Dublin, Ireland, and had a brother, John.

<u>Education</u>

Churchill was sent to boarding school at a young age but fared poorly academically. As a result, his father enrolled him into an army career at the Royal Military College, where he fared well.

<u>Early career</u>

In 1895, his father died, and Churchill joined the cavalry. In 1896, when he was a war correspondent in India, he ventured into writing books. Churchill left the army in 1899 to work as a war correspondent for the Morning Post. During his time at the Boer War, he was taken prisoner and made headlines with his escape to Portugal. He wrote another book about this experience.

Political career

Churchill became a member of the British Parliament with the Conservative Party in 1900. He followed his father's independence and was a supporter of social reform. When he felt unimpressed by the Conservative Party's commitment to social justice, he switched to the Liberal Party in 1904. In 1908, he was called to the prime minister's cabinet as president of the board of trade. At the board of trade, Churchill began his work by reforming the prison system, introducing the first minimum wage, and setting up unemployment insurance. He also helped to pass the budget, which introduced taxes on the rich to pay for new social welfare programs. In 1911, Churchill was made First Lord of the Admiralty. He went on to modernize the British Army by ordering new warships and setting up the Royal Navy Air Service

World War I

In 1915, Churchill resigned from the government because of his part in the Battle of Gallipoli - a disastrous attempt by the Allied Powers to control the sea route that resulted in heavy casualties.

Churchill was reappointed as minister of munitions in the final year of the war in 1917, whereby he supervised the production of airplanes, tanks, and munitions. After the war ended, he served as the minister of war and air, and colonial secretary under the prime minister. In 1922, Churchill rejoined the Conservative Party but was out of government with the party's defeat in 1929.

## Personal life

Churchill married Clementine Ogilvy Hozier in 1908, and they had five children. After his ousting from the government in the 1920s, Churchill painted over 500 paintings, working with portraits and still life. Throughout the 1930s, he focused on his writings.

## World War II (1940-1945)

The day Britain declared war on Germany in 1939, Churchill was reappointed as First Lord of the Admiralty. In 1940, Churchill became the chairman of the military coordinating committee. Churchill was appointed as prime minister and minister of defense by King George VI in 1940. Within hours of his appointment, Germany invaded Europe, and Britain stood alone. In 1941 after the Japanese attack on Pearl Harbor, Churchill went to Washington DC, and, along with President Franklin D. Roosevelt, allied to defeat Germany. Churchill led Britain through World War II until Germany's fall. He was an excellent wartime prime minister with his resilience and optimism, especially during the early defeats.

## Post-war

Despite Germany's defeat, Churchill lost in a general election in July 1945. Six years later, Churchill became the leader of the opposition party. In 1946, he made his famous Iron Curtain speech about Soviet domination while visiting the United

States. He became prime minister again in 1951 and went on to introduce domestic reforms such as the housing standards. Queen Elizabeth II knighted Churchill in 1953, and in the same year, he received a Nobel Prize for his six-volume history of World War II. He retired as prime minister in 1955 but remained as a member of parliament until 1964.

Death

At the age of ninety, Churchill died in his London home in 1965 after suffering a stroke. He was given a state funeral and buried in the family grave in Oxfordshire. Churchill's health problems started in 1941 when he first suffered a heart attack and a series of strokes after that. Despite his poor health, he remained active throughout his life.

The man himself

Churchill's lifetime spanned two World Wars. He was what Britain needed in her darkest hour of need. Churchill had a dogged determination, driving passion, and a cool-headed personality. Coupled with his ability to inspire while projecting optimism that instilled confidence in everyone, was the remarkable formula for his leadership success. It was no wonder he inspired the nation, and he has been hailed as the greatest Briton by the BBC.

## CHAPTER 3

# ABRAHAM LINCOLN

---

*"Most folks are about as happy as they make their minds up to be." -Abraham Lincoln*

**4 March 1861 - 15 April 1865**

Early life

Abraham Lincoln was born in Kentucky. His father was Thomas Lincoln, and his mother was Nancy. Lincoln had two siblings, but one died at infancy. His mother died when he was nine, leaving his older sister Sarah, eleven, in charge of the household. In 1819, his father remarried Sarah Johnston, and Lincoln was close to her. It was his stepmother that encouraged Lincoln in his love for reading.

Education

Both of Lincoln's parents were illiterate. Lincoln himself was primarily self-educated with little formal education. His entire schooling amounted to one year's attendance. Young Lincoln would travel miles to borrow books, somehow learning to read, and write by himself.

## As a young man

At twenty-one, Lincoln began life on his own. He was tall and lanky but physically strong. He spoke with a twang and was a good-natured man who attracted friends with his storytelling. At Illinois, he tried a variety of occupations ranging from a rail-splitter, a boatman to a postmaster.

## Early career

In 1834, Lincoln was elected to the Illinois state legislature as a member of the Whig Party. Around this time, he taught himself the law through reading. He was admitted to the bar in 1837 and began to practice in a law firm.

## Marriage

Lincoln married Mary Todd, a well-educated woman from a distinguished family in 1842. Together they had four sons, but only Robert Todd survived to adulthood.

## Political career

Lincoln served one term in the U.S. House of Representatives from 1847-1849. During his term, he spoke against the Mexican-American war, which made him very unpopular. He returned home to practice law. In 1856, Lincoln rejoined politics because of his views on slavery and his belief that all men were created equal with absolute rights. In 1858, Lincoln challenged the sitting U.S. Senator Stephen Douglas for his seat, and this led to seven stirring debates across different cities that were covered by the newspapers. The exposure launched Lincoln into national politics.

## As president

In 1860, Lincoln became the 16th U.S. President after receiving nearly a forty percent vote. He chose a cabinet that consisted of his longtime rivals, and he famously said, "Hold your friends close and your enemies closer." His cabinet was his strongest asset when he was in office.

## Civil war

The Civil War started in April 1861 after decades of tensions between northern and southern states over slavery. It was the bloodiest and costliest war fought on American soil. Lincoln responded by distributing $2 million from the treasury toward war material and asking for 75,000 volunteers without declaring war. During this time, the generals and cabinet were often at a disagreement with Lincoln.

In 1863, Lincoln delivered the Emancipation Proclamation, which stated that all slaves should be free in rebellious states such as Tennessee and the bordering states. He delivered his famous Gettysburg Address on 19 November 1863 at one of the bloodiest war sites. Lincoln invoked the principles of human equality and that all men are created equal.

<u>Death</u>

The Civil War ended in 1865, and Lincoln was re-elected for the presidency after winning a fifty-five percent vote. Unfortunately, before Lincoln could begin his post-war reconstruction policy, he was assassinated by John Wilkes Booth, a supporter of slavery, while attending a play at the theatre with his wife. Lincoln's death was mourned by millions in both the North and South.

<u>The man himself</u>

Historians have often cited Lincoln as America's greatest president because no other presidents have ever faced a greater crisis or accomplished so much. As a president, Lincoln effectively did everything in his power to ensure victory in the Civil War and to end slavery. Some have described Lincoln as a self-made man who rose from the lowest depths to the greatest heights. Health-wise, Lincoln was believed to have suffered from smallpox, malaria, and depression.

# CHAPTER 4

# MARGARET THATCHER

---

*"Being powerful is like being a lady. If you have to tell people you are, you aren't." -Margaret Thatcher*

**13 October 1925 - 8 April 2013**

<u>Early life</u>

Margaret Hilda Roberts was born in Lincolnshire, England. Her father, Alfred Roberts, and mother, Beatrice Stephenson, were middle class grocers. She had an older sister, Muriel. Her father also served as a town council member before becoming the mayor of Grantham in 1945.

<u>Education</u>

Thatcher was a hardworking student with extracurricular activities in hockey, swimming, piano, and poetry recitals. In 1943, Thatcher got a scholarship to Oxford, where she studied chemistry. After graduating, she worked as a research chemist, but her real interest was in politics.

## Politics and marriage

In 1950 and 1951, Thatcher ran for parliament and lost. She later married Denis Thatcher, a well-to-do businessman in December 1951, and they had twins. Around that time, she studied and passed the bar exams, spending the next few years practicing law.

In 1959, Thatcher ran and won a seat in the parliament. She became the parliamentary undersecretary to the Ministry of Pensions and National Insurance in 1961. She began moving up the ranks to become secretary of state for education and science. In 1975, she beat former Prime Minister Edward Heath and took leadership of the Conservative Party.

## Prime minister

The Conservative Party won the election in 1979, and Thatcher became England's first female prime minister. During her first term, she remedied England's recession by increasing interest rates. In 1982, Argentina invaded the Falkland Islands, and Thatcher sent troops to the area to end the fighting. Around that time, she and U.S. President Ronald Regan, a fellow conservative, became strong allies because of their shared right-wing political views and stand against the Soviet Union during the Cold War. Thanks to the war and improved economy, Thatcher won a second term from 1983-1987. In 1984, she escaped an assassination attempt by the Irish Republic Army.

## Fall from power

In 1987, Thatcher won her third election narrowly. However, her introduction of the poll tax, anti-European Union sentiments, and authoritarian style (she dismissed officials who opposed her) led her to be hugely unpopular among the public and within her party. On 22 November 1990, Thatcher resigned as prime minister after been ousted from her own party.

## Post politics

In 1992, Thatcher was appointed as Baroness Thatcher of Kesteven in the House of Lords. During this time, she wrote two books about her experiences as a world leader and lectured in the United States and Asia. She also established a Thatcher Foundation to support free enterprise and democracy.

## Later years

Thatcher retired from public speaking in 2002 after suffering minor strokes and symptoms of dementia. Thatcher eventually retreated and lived in near seclusion at her home in London until her passing at eighty-seven.

## The woman herself

Margaret Thatcher was famously known as the Iron Lady - a nickname for her uncompromising leadership style. Today she remains Britain's one and only female prime minister. Despite her humble background and being the youngest candidate, Thatcher dreamed big and nurtured ambitions in politics. Colleagues who interacted with her described Thatcher as a force of personality and almost too powerful for any rational discussion. One of her greatest assets was her in-depth comprehension of the aspirations of the working and middle class. Throughout her life, Thatcher had a singular passion for politics, and her secretary said, "She never had a happy day since leaving politics." Love her or hate her, Thatcher's decade of power had garnered her many admirers as well as haters.

## CHAPTER 5

# BILL CLINTON

---

*"We must teach our children to resolve their conflicts with words, not weapons." -Bill Clinton*

**19 August 1946 - Present**

<u>Early life</u>

William Jefferson Blythe III was born in Hope, Arkansas, three months after his father, William, passed away in an automobile accident. After he was born, his mother, Virginia, went to nursing school and later remarried Roger Clinton Sr. Clinton took his stepfather's surname when he was in high school.

<u>Education</u>

Clinton studied at Georgetown University in Washington, DC, and graduated with a degree in international affairs. In 1968, he was awarded a Rhodes scholarship to Oxford but left halfway to study law at Yale University. Like many young people during that time, Clinton opposed the Vietnam War. He received a draft deferment for the first year of university because of his scholarship. Later he tried to extend the deferment through Reserve Officers Training Corps; this created a controversy during his presidential campaign. Clinton admitted to experimenting with marijuana as a young man but claimed he didn't 'inhale' - this later became a topic of ridicule during his political career. After his graduation in 1973, Clinton returned to Arkansas to teach law at the University of Arkansas.

Politics and marriage

Clinton campaigned for a seat in the U.S. House of Representatives in 1974 but was unsuccessful. In 1975, Clinton married Hillary Rodham, a fellow law student from Yale. Their only child Chelsea was born in 1980.

In 1976, Clinton was elected attorney general of Arkansas. He became the governor of Arkansas in 1978, making him the youngest the country had seen in forty years. He lost the re-election in 1980 due to the unpopular decisions he had made. Two years later, Clinton regained governorship and served until 1993. During his twelve years as governor, Clinton received national recognition for his efforts to improve public education.

Presidency

In 1992, Clinton began his presidential campaign with Al Gore as his running mate. However, his campaign was nearly derailed by an alleged twelve-year affair with Gennifer Flowers. Clinton and his wife gave an interview on 60 Minutes admitting to some marital problems, and his popularity recovered. His famous statement, "I feel your pain," as his apparent sympathy for fellow

Americans, coupled with his personal charm won him the Democratic presidential nomination. He went on to challenge the incumbent president George Bush of Republican Party, and the independent candidate Ross Perot. Clinton eventually won with forty-three percent versus Bush at 37.4 percent and Ross at 18.9 percent.

Clinton's administration got off to a rocky start because of his campaign promise to end discrimination against gay men and lesbians in the military. Many conservatives, including General Colin Powel, criticized his administration. As a compromise, Clinton proposed the famous, "Don't ask, don't tell," policy which failed to address either party involved. He had successes with the North American free-trade agreement, the appointment of women and minorities to key roles in his administration, and the passing of significant bills pertaining to women and family issues. In 1994, Clinton and his wife were investigated for their role in the Whitewater housing development scandal, but there was no conclusive evidence found against them.

Clinton was re-elected as the U.S. 42nd president in 1996 at forty-nine percent vote thanks to the strong economic growth. However, his second term was overshadowed by the Monica Lewinsky scandal in 1998. At first, he repeatedly denied it before finally admitting to having sexual relations with his twenty-two-year-old intern, Lewinsky. This led to his impeachment, of which he was acquitted in 1999. Clinton apologized to his family and the American people. Despite the scandal, his popularity remained high, and he ended his presidency with a sixty-five percent approval rating.

## Life after presidency

Hillary Clinton won an elected office in 2000 as Clinton's presidency was ending. She went on to lose to Barrack Obama in the Democratic Party presidential nomination. Obama later appointed Hillary as the secretary of state during his administration. Clinton remained active politically and was a highly sought after speaker addressing various global issues such as AIDS and climate change. He even campaigned for Obama's second term in the White House. In 2016, Hillary Clinton entered the U.S. presidential race, with Clinton playing an active role in her campaign. However, she lost to Donald Trump.

According to Forbes, since leaving the White House, the Clintons raked in $240 million through writing books, speeches, and private consulting. Clinton himself made $38 million as an author with a bestselling memoir, 'My Life.' In 1997, they founded the Clinton Foundation, a non-profit humanitarian aid to tackle the world's challenges such as climate change, global health, and advocating opportunities for women.

## The man himself

At this point of writing, Clinton is seventy-four years old after surviving impeachment, open-heart surgery, and many personal and political challenges in his life. As a politician, he was known to be charismatic, personable, and highly persuasive to the effect that even his enemies would regularly be taken in by him. Clinton has a gift for making people feel special, understood, and cared for deeply. Wherever he campaigned, he was surrounded by a huge crowd of supporters. Despite his personal misstep, there is no denying the power of his personality and ability to make the Americans consistently trust him.

# CHAPTER 6
# BARACK OBAMA

---

*"Change will not come if we wait for some other person or some other time. We are the ones we've been waiting for. We are the change that we seek." -Barack Obama*

**4 August 1961 - Present**

Early life

Barack Hussein Obama II was born in Honolulu, Hawaii. His father, Barack Obama Sr. was an African from Kenya and mother, Ann Dunham; a European descendant who was an anthropologist. His parents met when studying at the University of Hawaii. Obama's parents divorced in 1964, and his father returned to Kenya, only returning once to see him. He later died in an automobile accident when Obama was twenty-one years old. In 1963, his mother remarried Lolo Soetoro an Indonesian and they moved to Indonesia in 1967 where Obama lived for four years

## Education

At ten, Obama returned to Hawaii alone and was raised by his maternal parents while studying in high school. In 1981, Obama entered Columbia University, where he graduated with political science and English literature degree. He went on to study law at Harvard Law School in 1988, where he graduated magna cum laude.

## Early career and marriage

After graduating, Obama worked at Business International Corporation and New York Public Interest Research Group. In 1992, Obama married a Chicago lawyer named Michelle LaVaughn Robinson. They met when he was working in the city as the director of the Developing Communities Project. Together they have two daughters Malia Ann and Natasha. During this time, Obama worked as a community organizer and taught at the University of Chicago Law School for twelve years.

## Politics

In 1996, Obama ventured into politics as a member of the Illinois State Senate. He was later elected to State Senate in 1998 and 2002. In 2004, Obama won as a state senator after positioning himself as a progressivist and anti-Iraq War. He became a rising star in the Democratic Party.

## Presidency

Obama began his presidential campaign in 2007. He was nominated by the Democratic Party after a close race against

Hillary Clinton. He named Joe Biden as his running mate, and the two campaigned with the message of hope and change. Obama's campaign was most notable for using digital strategy and raising a record of $750 million from small donors across the country. Obama became the U.S. 44th President in 2009, winning a 52.9 percent vote against Republican Senator John McCain. He was also U.S.' first African-American president.

During his first term, Obama signed the Recovery Act, which was a stimulus package that pumped $800 billion into the economy to help combat unemployment and ease further economic challenges. Obama's signature achievement was the Patient Protection and Affordable Care Act, known as Obamacare, which ensured all Americans have access to affordable healthcare.

In 2011, Osama Bin Laden, the mastermind of the September 11 terror attack, was killed during a Navy SEAL raid in Pakistan. This marked a major win for Obama as it was the country's most significant achievement against al Qaeda and a testament to the determination of the Americans.

Obama launched his re-election campaign in 2011 and hired a tech team that focused on digital campaign tools such as Facebook and Twitter. He won at 51.1 percent against Republican's Mitt Romney.

During Obama's second term, he faced new challenges such as Iran's nuclear weapons, gun violence following the mass shooting at Sandy Hook Elementary School in 2012, and the equal protection clause for same-sex marriage. In 2014, Obama became the first American president to visit Cuba after he announced plans to restore diplomatic relations with them. This move was met with approval by political leaders around the world.

## Life after presidency

On 20 January 2017, Obama stepped down as President and handed the job to Donald Trump. His post-presidency life kicked off with a vacation at one of the private British Virgin Islands where he was a guest of Sir Richard Branson. As civilians, he and Michelle, spent their time book writing and received an advance of $65 million from Penguin Random House for their memoirs. Apart from that, he was highly paid for speaking engagements - as much as $400,000 (double of what Clinton was paid). In 2018, the couple signed a deal to produce documentaries for Netflix under their production company Higher Ground Productions. At other times Obama went globetrotting with his family.

## The man himself

As a president, Obama's most significant legacy was his Obamacare. He also advanced LGBT rights when he signed the 'Don't Ask, Don't Tell' Repeat Act in 2010. When he left office, his approval rating was at sixty percent. In 2019, Obama and Trump tied as the most admired man in a Gallup poll - a spot Obama has held for twelve consecutive times. Obama was a prolific politician who earned the nickname, 'no drama Obama' for his cool temperament. He was a firm believer that if you believe something is right, you should take a stand and influence others with your message. He was big on change and tried to apply it in the way he ran the country. Obama was known to be a great speaker who had perfected the art of communication - he could talk to anyone, audience, or group regardless of their background. His entire presidential campaign was about communicating his message across to anyone eligible to vote.

# CHAPTER 7
# LEE KUAN YEW

---

*"I always tried to be correct, not politically correct."* -*Lee Kuan Yew*

**16 September 1923 - 23 March 2015**

<u>Early life</u>

Lee Kuan Yew was born in Singapore. His father was Lee Hoon Leong, and his mother was the second wife, Chua Jim Neo. Lee Kuan Yew had four siblings. Lee's grandparents were well-to-do, but their wealth declined during the Great Depression. His father was a depot manager at Shell, where he was given a house and a chauffeured car. Lee described his father as a man with a nasty temper and thus resolved to reign in his temper at a young age. It was Lee's mother that used her savings to pay for his education as his father had a gambling addiction. He credited his mother for holding the family together and standing up to his father even when he demanded she pawn her jewelry to pay for his gambling debts.

Early education

Lee attended the Telok Kurau English School but described his schoolmates as relatively poor and unintelligent. He later attended Raffles Institution in 1835, where he had difficulties keeping up with the top 150 students from the country. During his school years, Lee participated in debates, chess, tennis, and cricket. He won several scholarships, including one to Raffles College, where he met Kwa Geok Choo, his future wife. Kwa was an intelligent student who regularly topped Lee in English and economics.

World War II

World War II from 1942 - 1945 caused Lee's education to be delayed. Around that time, Lee learned the Japanese language so that he could survive as a Japanese translator. He also worked as a Singapore administration service officer at Sentosa Island. On the side, he set up a small enterprise manufacturing stationery glue. During the Japanese Occupation, Lee had a near-miss with death when he narrowly escaped the Sook Ching massacre. He recalled being slapped and forced to kneel for failing to bow to a Japanese soldier. Like many young Singaporeans at that time, Lee was determined that no one - British or Japanese had the right to push them around. Lee saw how the British failed to protect Singapore from the Japanese and decided that the country needed to govern itself.

England

After the war ended, Lee left for England to study at the London School of Economics but later switched to study law at Fitzwilliam College, a constituent college of the University of

Cambridge. He graduated first class and was called to the Bar at Middle Temple in 1950.

## Early career and marriage

After his return from England, Lee worked as a lawyer at John Laycock's firm. He was also the legal advisor to the students and trade unions. In 1951, Lee had his first experience with politics when he acted as an election agent for Laycock under the Progressive Party.

Lee married Kwa in 1950, and they had two sons and one daughter. As both of them spoke English as their first language, Lee started learning Chinese in 1955.

## Early politics

Singapore was previously a British colony that was used as a naval base in the Far East. In the 1950s, there were growing talks of independence and constitution reform among the people. Lee wanted to challenge the governing structure of Singapore and formed an alliance with two political newcomers. However, due to his radical stand, in 1954, he broke away from his original alliance and became secretary-general of his own party known as the People's Action Party (PAP).

In 1955, a new constitution was formed, and PAP won three seats versus the Labor Front, who won thirteen seats. The following year, Lee went to London to seek self-rule for the country, but he was unsuccessful. However, in 1957, negotiations in London restarted, and Lee won a by-election by an overwhelming majority. Shortly after, a power struggle ensued whereby Lee was ousted from PAP, but he managed to return four months later.

Back in London 1958, Lee negotiated for Singapore to be a self-governing state within the Commonwealth. Lee's party, the PAP, had a decisive win, and he was sworn in as prime minister on 5 June 1959. Lee formed a cabinet and introduced long-term plans for new public housing, education expansion, industrialization, and the emancipation of women. Around this time, Lee severed his remaining ties with the communists who used to support PAP.

In 1963, Singapore formed a merger with the Federation of Malaysia to gain independence from Britain. However, Lee made the mistake of entering PAP in the Malaysian national elections in 1963. This caused tensions between the Malays and Chinese resulting in race riots whereby hundreds were injured. In August 1965, Malaysia decided to sever all ties with Singapore and refused Lee's offer to work out a compromise. Lee was anguished by the failure of the merger as he believed it was crucial for Singapore's survival. As a result, Singapore became a sovereign state with Lee as her first prime minister.

Singapore independence

Lee launched a program to industrialize and strengthen the Singapore economy, knowing it was the key to survival as an independent country. He encouraged foreign investments and transformed the country into a major exporter of goods. At the same time, Lee also raised living and health standards for the people.

Lee continued to dominate the country's politics with PAP using an authoritarian style of government that occasionally infringed on civil rights. He was adamant about having a clean government and implemented anti-corruption measures such as paying salaries that matched the private sector. Under Lee's guidance, Singapore became second in per capita income and the chief financial center in Asia in the 1980s.

## Post prime minister

After serving thirty-one years as Singapore's prime minister, Lee stepped down as senior minister in 1990 and then later as minister mentor until 2011. His son Lee Hsien Loong became the third prime minister in 2004.

## Death

Lee passed away at ninety-one after a cardiac dysrhythmia.

## The man himself

It was no small feat to build a nation from scratch, and Lee no doubt achieved success by leaving behind a legacy of an efficiently run country that has a clean and centralized government. Lee's leadership style was described as a combination of fear and charisma. He was often criticized for his authoritarianism style and his suppression of the opposition parties. As a father, he was described by his children as being very strict but good. Lee was a unique leader and what Singapore needed at that time.

# CHAPTER 8
# MAHATHIR MOHAMAD

---

*"I don't care much whether people remember me or not. If people remember, well and good. If they don't remember, it's alright - I'm dead anyway." -Mahathir Mohamad*

**10 July 1925 - Present**

<u>Early life</u>

Mahathir bin Mohamad was born in Alor Setar, the capital of Kedah, Malaysia. His father, Mohamad Iskandar was a school teacher, and his mother was Wan Tempawan. He had eight siblings.

<u>Education</u>

Mahathir was a hardworking student, but he showed little interest in sports. He won a scholarship and was fluent in English ahead of his schoolmates. During the Japanese Occupation, when the schools were closed, he went into small business selling coffee, banana fritters, and snacks. After the war, he graduated from secondary school and went on to study medicine at the King Edward VII College of Medicine in Singapore in 1946.

## Marriage

Mahathir met his wife, a fellow medical student, Siti Hasmah Mohamad Ali, at college. They married in 1956 and had seven children.

## Career

After graduating in 1953, Mahathir worked as a government medical doctor. In 1957, at thirty-two, he went into private practice and became his town's first Malay physician. He had a large house built, invested in businesses, and was chauffeured by a Chinese instead of the usual Malay.

## Politics

Mahathir became involved in politics toward the end of Japanese occupation. In 1964, he was elected to parliament as a member of the dominant party United Malays National Organization (UMNO). He was later expelled from UMNO in 1969 for advocating Malay nationalism and writing the book 'The Malay Dilemma,' which brought him into conflict with the prime minister, Tunku Abdul Rahman. Mahathir was reinstated in 1972, and around that time, his career took off. In 1974, he was promoted to a cabinet position and rose to deputy prime minister in 1976.

Prime minister

In July 1981, Mahathir became the first commoner to become prime minister in Malaysia. He exercised caution in his first two years and had battled for more authority among the royal family. Under his leadership, Malaysia experienced rapid economic growth and progressive changes to its culture and government. However, during the 1990s recession, Malaysia's economy entered a depression, causing a rift between Mahathir and his apparent successor deputy prime minister, Anwar Ibrahim - who supported international and open markets versus Mahathir who mistrusted the west. In 1998, Anwar was dismissed and charged with corruption and sodomy, causing protests, which called for Mahathir's resignation. Mahathir suppressed Anwar's supporters and consolidated his power.

To the west, Mahathir was a controversial figure, and he had complicated relationships with the United States, Britain, and Australia because of his criticisms of their policies. In Malaysia, he banned The Wall Street Journal and New York Times for writing negative reports about him.

Mahathir retired as prime minister in 2003 after twenty-two years in power. In 2008, he retired from UMNO and withdrew from the party.

Retirement

During his retirement, Mahathir wrote several books, including his memoirs in 2011. He was also an advisor to many flagship Malaysian companies such as Proton and Petronas. However, in the wake of the 1Malaysia Development Berhad (1MDB) scandal in 2015, he returned to politics to criticize his former protégé and then Prime Minister Najib Razak for his involvement in a $700 million financial scandal.

## Oldest prime minister

In 2018, Mahathir and Anwar put aside their longstanding rivalry to stand together against Najib. Mahathir announced his candidacy for prime minister and stunned the world by winning the general election, making him the oldest prime minister in the world at the age of ninety-three. Meanwhile, Najib was charged for embezzlement and money laundering activities.

Two years later, Mahathir had resigned as prime minister on 24 February 2020 to honor his promised handover to Anwar as his successor. However, Anwar did not hold enough seats to form a government. Instead, Muhyiddin Yassin, who had the majority vote, became the 8th prime minister of Malaysia on 1st March 2020.

## The man himself

Mahathir may be a controversial figure to the west, but to others, he is the voice of freedom for smaller countries that are squeezed by the imperialism of the east and west. In a way, Mahathir is a true independent spirit who is not afraid to speak his mind even on international levels. As prime minister, he was a visionary leader who successfully transformed Malaysia into a social and economic model for the Muslim world. As a man who despises brutality, Mahathir frequently championed world issues such as the plights of the Rohingyas and Palestinians. To date, many Malaysians highly regard his vast experience and respect him as a great statesman.

# CONCLUSION

Thank you for reading this book.

I hope this book has been an eye-opener giving you a glimpse into the lives and minds of the world's great leaders from across the ages. Perhaps their life stories might even inspire you to take the next step toward your success story.

Yours truly,

**LEE KHENG CHOOI**

www.ingramcontent.com/pod-product-compliance
Lightning Source LLC
Chambersburg PA
CBHW030543290526
45786CB00004B/1844